Curiosity is like addiction, it is never satisfied.

Let your mind wander to the possibilities of what nature has in mind for your life, then plan on using this new knowledge as you acquire its meanings.

--

CYCLES & RHYTHMS OF INTRIGUE

CYCLES, TO AN INQUIRING MIND, IS FASCINATION

By

Donald L. Boone

INTRODUCTION

Astrologers are often looked upon with great awe, as if a magician, or a Shaman. In reality there is no mystery about Astrologers, they are simply people who have taken it upon themselves to study the science of Astrophysics in some depth. To an Astrologer this becomes a religion of study. In truth, anyone can explain the coming events to some degree with knowledge of many basic cycles, or rhythms of life. A cycle is an event that goes full circle, something that returns to its point of origin. A Rhythm is something that continues the same way each time, but may not return to the exact point of origin.

Some of the early pioneers in cycle research are, Dr. Hyde Clark - 1838 who found cycles in the business community. A few more are, Samuel Benner, 1875 and the cycle of prices, Ernest Thompson Seton, an American Naturalist who studied the cycles of animal population, and my favorite, Edward R. Dewey, who wrote a book on the subject of Cycles. It was his book that drew me into the study of rhythms and cycles. It has proved an adventure of its own.

You will find a list of many items in this book, it may seem extensive, but it is merely a fraction of those cycles and rhythms to be found and yet explored. Some may seem to be short in duration, but can prove to have a long term affect. You will not find astronomical solutions to every cycle or rhythm in this book.

There are many more cycles that I could ascertain as to how they come about, or behave, according to the methods I use for my research.

There will be those in life who scoff at this kind of Astronomical research, but ignorance of truth has been with us for some time. These kinds of believers could easily have been like the founders of the 'Flat Earth' society. Yet, under pressure they will admit that the moon does affect the ocean's tides, and of course they know people have a heart beat, and yes there are seasons each year. They realize that the Sun does seem to have sun spot cycles. Still, they deny it affects mankind.

Read what interests you in this book, compare it to your life, or events that you are familiar with, then you too will become a believer in 'Cycles and Rhythms.'

There is another cycle factor to consider and that is that each ting listed in this book has some kind of beginning. Many people do not think far enough ahead to put that thought into perspective, that all things have a birth time. The life span may be long, or it may be quite short, but the birth influences are put in place at the time it all starts. Some may be difficult to think of as a life span because we do not think of corn as having a life. It does, as do bugs or rocks, or whatever else you might think of.

3

Another important factor that needs to be considered when you read about cycles is that they involve planetary influences. These cycles and rhythms are often listed in such a manner as to use the mean average distance, or time traveled between the high and low points.

As with many cycles, they may not be easily found without in-depth research. The normal cycle of events taking place may also be affected by more than one planetary influence. This will result in different highs, and lows. Also, if a cycle, or rhythm is interrupted by some other event, the cycle will resume its original form when that influence has ceased to exist. The alternating circumstance affecting these cycles is often the Retrograde, or Direct motion of the planet that rules the event, and most often the location of the Moon's Nodes.

A situation often overlooked by those doing basic research, is how other cycles intercept one another. As an example, a very important time in most people's lives is at the age of 28, 29. What happens at this time is that many people start on an entirely new direction in life. The more important cycles that are in effect at this time are these.

First, you have the planet Uranus involved and it is trine to the natal location at that time. The effect of Uranus is to cause a change and it doesn't care what kind, but it will be for the better. Then you have a Saturn return at the same time. It will do the sub-conscience bidding, so the change will take place that is needed mentally as well.

In addition you have the Moon's nodal influence. It is at the nodal age of 28 and it too will have an effect, this one is more of an emotional level. So, in all cycles you must remember that you are normally only dealing with the rudimentary cycle of that planetary body in space, but that influence can be altered by other planets that may change things on a temporary basis. After that influence passes, the normal cycle will return.

Personal Cycles

When it comes to understanding how each person is affected by a cycle you will need a natal birth chart on that individual. With this information you can see how and where each cycle has an affect, or impacts their lives. If you are looking for answers as to how a relationship between two people is affected, you will need a chart for when those two people came together. Such as in a marriage, the time, date and place it took place will be the birth of that relationship. It need not be a marriage, it can be any kind of partnership that started at a particular point in time.

Though the author of this book resides in the United States, the cycles contained within these pages can be used for reference, or research, for any location on earth.

CYCLE CONTENTS

Addicts & Addiction . . .10
Accidents 12
Air craft flights . . .12
Birds of a feather . . .13
Birth cycles 14
Board games . . .14
Building construction . .15
Changing Partners . . .15
Chess Players . . .16
Church offerings . . .17
Church Membership . .18
Corn prices 19
Cotton prices . . .20
Creative Cycles . . .21
Civilization cycles . . .22
Crime cycles . . .23
Cycles of Mankind . . .24
Cyclic Years 26
Death cycles . . .27
Dog bites 27
Dress lengths . . .28
Earths Axis 28
Earth Cycles 28
Earth Quakes . . .29
Earths warming & cooling cycles .30
Eclipse cycles . . .31
El Nino, or La Nina . . .31
Emotional Blackmail . .33
Energy cycles . . .34
European wheat prices . .35

Evening Grosbeak . . .35
Farm crops 36
Full Moons 36
Grass Hoppers . . .37
Great Lakes Water Levels . .37
Heart disease . . .37
Ice age 38
Immigration levels . . .39
Injured fingers and toes . .39
Levels of Sub-conscience . .40
Life Changing Nodal Returns .41
Life Insurance sales . .42
Lunar Phases . . .43
Mass Excitement Cycle . .44
Marriage 46
Menstrual Cycles . . .47
Mentality 48
Mercury 49
Metal production . . .49
Metonic Cycle . . .50
Mice 50
Mid-life crisis . . .51
Moon 51
Moon's Nodes by age . .52
New Beginnings . . .53
Nodal Returns . . .54
Planetary Orbits . . .55
Plankton 57
Railroads 57
Real Estate Sales . . .58
Sales cycles 59
Salmon cycle . . .59
Saturn cycles . . .60

Sexual cravings . . .61
Sexual advertising . . .62
Sexual predators . . .63
Solar radiation. . . .63
Stock prices 64
Suicide 65
Sun 66
Suns polarity . . .67
Sun spots 68
Tires shredding . . .70
Traveling 71
Trees 72
Uranus cycle . . .73
War cycles 74
Weather cycles . . .76
Wheat Prices . . .77
Writer's block . . .78
Researcher's planetary info. 84 to 98
Glossary 95

ADDICTS & ADDICTION OF ANY KIND
The interest in this cycle began when an Astrological client asked me why she was addicted to sex. I knew it had to involve the first house of her horoscope as that represents the physical body. It also had to involve Venus as it rules the need to give, and receive love, or pleasures.

Then I considered the constellations that were the strongest possibilities for sexuality. Those four are, Scorpio, Capricorn, Aquarius, and Aries. It is the constellation Venus is in at the time a person is born that tells the story of how the addiction affects each individual.

However, when the planet Venus is found in the first house the addiction will be, for the most part, physical pleasure. This also brings about over indulgence of any kind. Those who suffer the greatest addictions are often found to be born in the winter months. October to April, the worst of these are October, December, February, and April.

When the Moon passes through the same constellation that Venus was in at birth, the addiction becomes the strongest for satisfying the need. It has been noted that as the moon, in its monthly transit, is the trigger effect in our lives.

Whatever astrological house that Venus is in at the time of birth can indicate how the addiction may play a part in each person's life, whether it is physical, mental or emotional.

Neptune and its mental illusions can be a part of addiction, as can planets in the twelfth house which can be influenced by Neptune. The placement of Venus at the time of birth, and its relationship with Mars and Saturn can show how the addiction takes place as it represents the pleasures taken in life whether they are beneficial to us, or not.

ACCIDENTS

Personal accidents seem to happen more often when the transiting moon is in a sign opposite to the location of the moon at the time of a person's birth. This was found in a report from Sandia Laboratories in New Mexico and from information gleaned from their personnel records.

AIRCRAFT FLIGHTS

These have a high and low of 5.5 years and have been studied since 1930. You will find that the high points of travel by aircraft seem to be when the planet Mercury is in Aquarius, which influences air travel. This is the sign on the third house in the chart for the USA, a house of short distance travel. And it appears in Leo, of the ninth house, for the low travel point. Traveling by aircraft is, by most people, considered a short trip, thus the third house influence. However, there is another influence that affects the high and low points of this cycle, and that is the Retrograde, or Direct, condition of Mercury, and that of its declination. When it turns to the north from a south declination, or when it turns south from a north declination. This can be a difficult cycle to investigate as information concerning years of the past are not readily available.

BIRDS OF A FEATHER
It is known that most bird populations change size depending upon the abundance of their food supplies, but their food supplies are also found to occur in cycles. The Northern Shrike, the rough-legged hawk and the Snowy Owl have three to five years changes in their populations on average. The Pine Grosbeak has a five to six-year cycle and the Horned Owl has a cycle of nine to eleven years. I believe these are all tied to the planet Saturn. For years the Sooty Tern drove the US Air Force crazy. It seems that in 1942 they built an airfield right in the center of its nesting area without knowing the small web footed creatures would return to that location every 9.7 months to lay its over sized eggs.

The more prominent cycles will take place on the squares and oppositions to that of when the bird, or flock of birds was born. However, the Downy Woodpecker, the Hairy Woodpecker and the Bob White cycles change every 50.7 months, this would be to the square aspect of Saturn from the time of birth. I realize you will not know the birth data of a flock of birds, but this is a fact as real as any other. The Bob White does things a little differently, and they are always found close to home, even in death.

BIRTH CYCLES

Everything that begins anew, whether it is the birth of a child, the birth of an animal in the forest, the beginning of a marriage, any kind of relationship, or simply the birth of an idea, will have some kind of cycle affecting its life as time passes. This is one of the reasons that Astrologers need the time, date, and place for when any event started. With this information they can tell you its future, for the most part. As to the time the births take place, hospital records indicate that more births take place on the waxing phase of the moon than on the waning phase of the moon. Also, more males are born during the waxing moon phase.

BOARD GAMES

The popularity of board games seems to come back every 14 years. If the game is unusual enough, it can make inroads into the community. This may be part of the Uranus cycle, but this like other cycles would depend upon the time the game was actually formed.

BUILDING CONSTRUCTION
These have been studied since 1939 and average
33 months in length. Building construction
generally follows the housing market. Thus, it has
a 9.2 year cycle as well. When the housing
market is going up, those who speculate on the
selling new home's, construct them as fast as
they can. Many contractors speculate on the
housing market but not necessarily to out guess
the current housing needs, but more to keep their
better workers busy so that they will continue
working for their current contractors as skilled
craftsmen.

CHANGING PARTNERS
Mankind in general tends to seek a new mate
periodically. Typically it follows an 8.9 year cycle,
and this happens regardless of the condition of
their current marital or mated status. To
investigate this kind of activity, look to the moon's
nodal positions in a person's natal chart. When
they reach the south node, by age, they may
begin to search for a new mate. This is not
necessarily done to replace the one they are
currently involved with, just one that is different.
This will fall in line with the cycle of Uranus, as it
wants a change of some kind.

CHESS PLAYERS

It seems as if chess champions are more often born when the Moon's North Node is in the fire signs of Aries, Leo, or Sagittarius. The more prominent position is when it is in the constellation of Aries, as this is the aggressor and ruler of war. The cycles for this run on an average of every 18 to 20 years. The only written records of this I have come across are found in chess books related to chess history. Many list the birth dates for the players themselves, and out of curiosity I found the better players to be born under these conditions. The sun signs of the players' themselves differ from player to player.

CHURCH OFFERINGS

Donations for the church, or relief programs would normally be due to the planet Jupiter, as it rules the ninth house and that of the hierarchy of Theology. Most cycles involve the Moon, or its influence in some manner. This cycle also has the Lunar influence, but it is slightly different. Its influence comes from the Elements of Fire, Earth, Air and Water. The normal cycle of funding the churches needs from the pockets of the public, come in 3.5 year cycles. The alternating circumstance affecting these cycles can be the Retrograde, or Direct motion of Jupiter.

The Moon's Nodal involvement comes through the element that the Moon's Node is in each time of the change. The fire signs control the life of the church itself, and what you are taught to believe in. The Air signs are the communicating with the church's followers, and friends. The Earth signs have influence in the church's wealth, its funding or helping others, and its business. This would include the members tithing's to the church. Some label this as 'Conscience money.' The water signs concern the church as a home for those in need of spiritual guidance, ceremonies and mortality.

CHURCH MEMBERSHIP

In 1950 Pastor Harold Martin revealed his findings to Edward R. Dewey, the author of the book, 'Cycles,' which was published in 1971. He presented charts of his research that spanned a hundred years, or better. It included records for the Methodist, Episcopal, Presbyterian, and Congregational denominations.

He'd discovered that membership in the churches' rose for four and a half years, and then fell for four and a half years, all in all a nine-year cycle. Though his records did not include the other churches around the world, it is believed that the same cycle applies to them as well. To see how this works, look at the Moon's North Node at a high point in Libra in January 1940. At four and a half years later, the North Node is in Cancer in 1944, a squared aspect to the high point of 1940. Its next high point comes at the opposition in Aries in 1949. The next low was when the North Node was in Capricorn in 1954. The next two recorded highs took place when the North Node was in Libra in June 1958, and in Aries in November 1967.

CORN PRICES
The records of the 3.5 year cycle and the 3.5 to 3.75 year cycle, can be traced back to 1720, and are still available to the present time. Though it may have a rhythm that runs on an average for several years, it has been known to change periodically. The cycle is affected by the planting time of each crop. This is also affected by the season and the country within which it is planted. However, if you consult an Ephemeris at the time of year that the corn crops are planted in your area, you will find the cycle reaches its high, or low point, when the moon node is squared by aspect to the original dates on the 3.5 year cycle. The 3.75 year cycle takes place when the Moon's node is Trine by aspect to the beginning dates. There is yet another cycle concerning corn. Samuel Benner, discovered a 5.5 year fluctuation that takes place on occasion.

COTTON PRICES

It was found that keeping a record of the average 17.75 year cycles of cotton prices were started in 1740, with a record high at 1750, and that the records were kept until 1945. These are of course, forced cycles. That is the growth cycle persists, but is controlled by weather before mankind can take over the control of the prices.

These may be related to the planet Saturn, the sign it is in at the time of the high prices, but dependent on the other outside forces, weather and demand. There is another factor to consider as well. You may find more demand, and higher prices, when Saturn is Retrograde in its orbit, and lower demand and prices when it is in Direct motion in its orbit.

I found two recorded highs listed. One was in 1904 when Saturn was in Aquarius, and another in 1920 when it was in Virgo. You may want to consider the fact that this cycle closely resembles the marriage cycle, which involves the Moon's Nodes.

On rare occasion an unusual cycle may appear around 6.0, 9.0, or 12.0 years. You might refer to the Moon's Nodes by age at the back of this book.

CREATIVE CYCLES

There are gaps that take place in the creative cycles of those with an artistic ability. The shorter ones lasts about three weeks each time and this takes place three of four times a year. This is found to coincide with the same time period that the planet Mercury is in a retrograde condition.

The better part of the short cycle seems to be the last week, as it is a period where the mind brings forth many new ideas to work on. You will hear writers referring to this entire time period as, 'Writer's Block.' But, it does not pertain to just writers.

There is another cycle of 7.6 months that seems to have some affect, and may be due to the Moon's influence and which constellations it is passing through at the time. This will be a different time period for each person.

Another possible contributing influence could be that of Mercury going through an opposition to its natal location at birth, or of the productive planets shown in the persons birth chart. This would be the planet Venus, Mercury, or a combination of those planets with the power in the chart. It could also include planets in the sections of a persons life known as power locations in the birth chart.

Another cycle that is of importance is one of seven years in duration. All may go well as the artistic ability shows itself in the work of those producing something of value from within. However, when this cycle slows, or even stops, a seven-year stoppage can be devastating to the artistic talent, no matter what that talent is. Some may just give up pursuing their natural ability, and then only dabble in it as a pleasurable past time.

This cycle is most likely linked to the planet Uranus. The orbit of Uranus is eighty-four years but can be tracked in seven year segments starting at the time of birth. Each seven-year segment can bring about a change in some manner.

CIVILIZATION CYCLES
This is a cycle that corresponds to the conjunction of Jupiter and Saturn. It seems that civilizations can be born, and die, in the span of 794 years.

CRIME CYCLES

J. Edgar Hoover, of the Federal Bureau of Investigation, was a strong believer in crime cycles and he was certain they could be predicted. I guess it really isn't a surprise that the types of crimes that take place are seasonal. Murder reaches its high point during July and August. This of course is when the Sun is in its natural sign of Leo, the ruling sign of life. Negligent manslaughter is lowest between May and mid September. Its high periods are during the darker, colder months of October through March. However, rape and aggravated assault are highest in July and lowest in January. Murder, however, is a weekend crime and 63% of them take place at nighttime between 6:00 P.M. and 6:00 A.M.. Robbery is different, it has the highest possibility of taking place between 6:00 P.M. and 2:00 A.M.. Also it happens more often on Saturday night and in the months of December, January, or February. Auto theft is at its highest in the middle of February and early November. Its lowest point during the years is from late July through the middle of September. The safest month from crime is during the month of May. The moon, of course, is the main triggering of these crimes, but the crimes themselves will be products of other planets, such as those having to do with each kind of emotion, like Mars, Venus, and Mercury.

CYCLES OF MANKIND

Though Mankind can be dated back to 3.6 or 3.8 million years ago. The prehistory of our current phase of mankind could have started this time around 10,500 BC. There are few, if any, of those who research the beginning of mankind in such a manner as finding out how we, as human beings, actually of where we came from in the beginning.

There are several schools of thought on this subject, and many make each different believer angry over what seems obvious to each others point of view. In my opinion, it is ludicrous to think that we evolved from apes when there is so much pointing to another solution. I know, I know, You may believe in Darwin's theory of evolution, and to some extent he is correct, but he was dealing with species already present, just relocated to other areas.

This is not the case with mankind, though we did evolve and adapt, it was more to cope with the environments we found as we began to roam around the world.

Instead of searching for our ancestry from known times, we need to explore the times beyond and before those we have recorded. We are currently exploring the possibility of traveling to distant planets, such as Mars.

We've already been to our own moon, and the hunger is to go farther into the universe. Why are we so mentally restricted that we cannot fathom the idea that the first of our kind, in whatever form, came from elsewhere?

There are those who think we came originally from Osiris in Orion's belt. This idea is substantiated by history as we know it. Such as the layout of the great pyramids, the statues on Easter Island that stare into the sky, and many other known religions that worships the Gods from the heavens.

Even one of our own books on history tells us of the great Gods and the struggles of mankind's survival in the beginning. When you read this book of knowledge, read it and interpret it to your own understanding, not what someone else tells you while they stand on a pulpit. I'm referring to the 'Old Testament.' When it mentions a mother delivering 700 children, it is not speaking of childbirth as we know it.

CYCLIC YEARS

The years involved with cycles are too numerous to list here, but the one that carries the most intrigue is 9.2 years. There is a corresponding cycle involving the water level in Lake Michigan, or in the prices of pig iron which have been kept since 1784. In the Rincon Mountains of Arizona, the tree rings seem to be thicker at 9.2 year intervals.

There are more Partridges found in Hertfordshire, England on this cycle. Grass hopper abundance increases, Auto sales, Lake levels, Patents issued, and stock prices. The list of those cycles falling between 9.2 years and 9.7 years are simply too numerous to list here.

DEATH CYCLES

Studies on this subject were started in 1860 and the highest and lowest points are separated by 8.92 year span of time. This too, is a lunar cycle.

I've found it interesting to compare family death rates, by average age of those in the family who have passed on, to the location of the Moon's Nodes in the natal chart of those individuals. The node closest to that average age period of the family may be an indication of one's own death period.

You can figure this out by starting at the first house cusp and adding two years four months for each house. Go around the chart until that node is reached by age. A doctor Petersen in Chicago found that more deaths occur seven days after the full moon and the least deaths occur eleven days before.

DOG BITES

Dog bites seem to reach their peak in May. It may be because the sun is found in the sign of Taurus at that time. A sign of possessiveness, and if you are found to be in their area of domain, you may be faced with a possessive animal.

DRESS LENGTHS

We all know that there are clothing wars going on constantly between designers around the world, but, odd as it may seem, the length of a woman's dress has a long term cycle of changing every 100 years.

EARTH'S AXIS

The earth's axis cycle completes one full cycle every 26,000 years. The magnetic poles follow a cycle as well. They rotate on a 41,000 year cycle, which involves a tilt from 22.1 degrees to 24.5 degrees. This is more commonly called the 'Wobble.' This tilting of the axis will also affect other cycles as the earths north or south hemispheres are closest to the sun.

EARTH CYCLES

It is believed that the next time the earth's magnetic poles are expected to change is 2030. This could bring about extreme catastrophes. It is believed that the earth will suffer some problems 18 years before that time.

EARTH QUAKES

This in itself, is an on going study, to the extent that I will not attempt to cover it here. However, it seems there is a correlation between the eleven year sunspot's cycle and earthquakes. The averages fall about 10.96 years apart. Some studies, by Charles Davidson, date back to 1305, his work continued until 1899. During that period of time there were 53 peaks of high earthquake activity at an average of 10.96 years apart.

I've no doubt there is a lunar influence as well, and one that coincides with the Nodal age. However, you may want to consider the influence of Jupiter as well. Cycles concerning earth quakes also seem to depend on what part of the world you are studying at the time.

There are a few known cycles of 11.0 years, one of 17.66 years, 33 years and 134 years for a longer cycle. You should keep in mind that as the earths crust cools, the seismic activity will continue to change and so will the cycles of earthquakes.

EARTH'S WARMING AND COOLING CYCLES

One cooling cycle, investigated by John Imbrie, is believed to have started 6,000 years ago, and to complete its 19,000 year cycle, it will continue to cool for another 13,000 years.

However, a recent study by Berger and Loutre, suggests that the current warming trend could last another 50,000 years.

Recently someone who researches the Sun, and its effects, found that the Sun is actually the culprit for the earths getting warmer, and that it is not the fault of mankind.

ECLIPSE CYCLES

The following list summarizes various eclipse cycles.

Cycle	Days	Years
Fortnight	14.77 days	0.043
Month	29.53	0.085
Semester	177.18	0.511
Lunar Year	354.37	1.022
Octon	1387.94	4.004
Octaeteris	2923.53	8.434
Tritos	3986.63	11.501
Saros cycle	6585.32	18.999
Metonic cycle	6939.69	20.021
Inex	10,051.95	30.500
Exeligmos	19,755.96	56.996
Callippic cycle	27,259	80.085
Hipparchic	126,007.2	363.531
Babylonian	161,177.95	464.999
Tetradia	214,038.72	617.500

El NINO, OR La NINA

This warming trend of the sea usually takes place in the Pacific Ocean in late December and off the west coast of South America. It can have a marked influence as it takes place. Sir Gilbert Thomas Walker wrote about it in 1923, and Captain Camilo notified the National Geographic Society Congress about it in Lima Peru in 1892.

There seems to be a correlation between these cycles that fall within the Moon's Nodal ages. North or south declination of the moon does not seem to have an effect. There is some concern about the polar cap ice melting, as it has been for centuries, but that a rapid meltdown could affect the ocean's currents which are often responsible for the climate changes in different parts of the world.

EMOTIONAL BLACKMAIL
This is an ongoing condition and is often found to increase during times of stress in the world. It will be of no surprise for those who know something about astrology, and that is that blackmail is influenced by the planet Neptune and its home constellation of Pisces and the twelfth house of the Zodiac.

In the past few years Neptune is found to inhabit the constellation of Aquarius, the natural sign for humanitarian issues. The twelfth house often keeps things hidden, or at least out of sight of those who do not do the work to look into the reality of supposedly charitable organizations. When the moon's north node passes through the constellation of Aquarius those who prey on the masses are abundantly available. The high side of the cycle is when the moon's north node is in the constellation of Aquarius. The low side is when the moon's node is found in the constellation of Leo.

As you know, many so-called charities are little more than fronts for making an income for those who control said charities with little actually going out to those they are said to represent.

Examples of emotional blackmail can be found in advertisements that take place almost daily. Such as those that tell you that you should purchase insurance, or gold to protect your wealth. Perhaps offer to lend you money against your home, only for you to discover that you no longer own the home. These are, in a sense, legal theft. Neptunian illusions are used against us as individuals.

ENERGY CYCLES

Each person has an energy cycle and it starts at the time of birth. From that point on the highest energy takes place every year. The first one is at the age of 11 ½ months, or 343 days after birth. The low energy points take place mid way between those dates.

There is another cycle that intersects this one, and one that can carry a more life altering impact. This is an 11.88 year cycle. The highs and lows are listed as follows for most people's lives. From birth they are.

High	Low
Birth	5.94 years
11.88 years	17.82 years
23.76 years	29.7 years
35.64 years	41.58 years
47.52 years	53.46 years
59.54 years	65.34 years
71.28 years	77.22 years
81.16 years	87.1 years
93.04 years	98.98 years

EUROPEAN WHEAT PRICES

The wheat prices follow a 54 year cycle Records for this can be found dating back as far as 1259 and was discovered by Lord Beveridge. In my research of this cycle I found it seems to follow a Uranus cycle. It does not always follow an exact 54 year cycle, and it alters a year or two on occasion. Also, it seems the higher prices take place when Uranus is in Gemini, Libra, Aquarius, Cancer, Scorpio or Pisces. The lowest prices occur when Uranus is in Taurus, Virgo, Capricorn, Aries, Leo, or Sagittarius.

EVENING GROSBEAK

This is a small North American bird, but it is one with an unusual habit. It returns to New England during its migration. However, normally only every other year, and usually on the odd-numbered years. This occurrence has been known about since 1913. They also miss a year on occasion. Even if something affects their normal rhythm they will return to the established cycle.

FARM CROPS

The cycle on farm crops is reported to be 9.6 years, however, it has not always been steadfast on a continual basis. The basic cycle suggests that the highest, and lowest production occurs when the Moon's nodes are in earth signs, Taurus, Virgo and Capricorn. When this cycle deviates the cause could be from another planet as there seems to be an influence from Saturn as well. With Saturn involved we see the high, and low acreage production takes place when Saturn is often found to be trine to its last position of a high or low point, and when the farms were producing large and bountiful crops.

FULL MOON'S

The size of the full moon varies depending on where it is in its orbit around the earth. If it is near the earth, in its perigee, and it seems larger. If it is farther out in its orbit, which is its apogee, it seems smaller. The phase the moon is in, and its illumination depends on its placement in its orbit with respect to the sun. One half of the moon is illuminated by the sun all of the time, with the exception of eclipses. Depending on the observer's location on earth and it depends on how much of the illuminated surface of the moon can be seen.

GRASS HOPPERS
You might wonder how grass hoppers can have a cycle, but of course they do. Their cycles are dependent on the food they seek, which of course are the farm crops. It differs slightly as it is recorded for being 9.2 years in length. One of 15 years, and one of 22.7 years. It is the 9.2 year cycle that captures the imagination the most, because that cycle is found in several other things in our lives as well.

GREAT LAKES WATER LEVEL
It seems there is a 22.75 year cycle involved in the water levels in the Great Lakes. This was found by Colonel Harry A. Musham of Chicago in the 1940s, and Lake Michigan has another cycle of 9.2 years.

HEART DISEASE
With a cycle of 9.6 to 9.8 years you will have to look at the Moon's nodes in each person's natal chart, and the related planets as to each individual's potential for health problems. However this cycle has been continually tracked in the United States and reaches a high and low on those cyclic years. This cycle could have a Saturn cycle involved, and may be linked to the Sun spot cycles as well.

ICE AGE

The term 'Ice Age' is related to the science of Glaciology. This implies extensive ice sheets and with this in mind we are still in an ice age because Greenland and the Antarctic still have ice sheets. The current ice age, of which we are nearing its end, it started about 20 million years ago, and this was not even a full ice age. As to the cause of ice ages, the discussions on this subject are huge in number. To say mankind is responsible is to show ignorance. It is believed that we have had at least four Ice ages, and all of them have taken place before our time on earth began. The earths tilt at the axis are believed to be a part of the forming of ice sheets as the poles do not receive enough sunlight to keep them warm enough to prevent ice from forming. You can find some information on this in the 'Earths Axis' cycle.

IMMIGRATION LEVELS
The amount of people seeking protection, or
asylum from their native homelands, in the USA,
or any other country by seeking status as an
immigrant, has a cycle of 18.2 years since the
nineteenth century. This could be tied to their own
natal chart and the nodal returns of the moon.
This is the same cycle as that of the marriage
cycle. In a sense this relationship is similar as
they are seeking changes in their personal lives.

INJURED FINGERS AND TOES
Recently while speaking with a hospital
emergency room nurse, I found that the hospital
has periodic increases in injuries to fingers and
toes and that this happens about three or four
times a year. In tracking these particular increases
I found they correspond to the planet Mercury
going into a retrograde condition. It seems the
increase is more prominent going into the second
week of the retrograde condition. The retrograde
Mercury cycle usually lasts an average of three
weeks.

LEVELS OF SUB-CONSCIENCE EVENTS

This a cycle that is rarely noticed by anyone, probably because it is acted out by the sub-conscience mind.

From birth until about the age of 14 years nine months, life is just experienced. From that age until the age of 29 and a half years, the mind is beginning to think it does not have to accept the seemingly normal status of how things are the way they are. At this age some major changes in a person's life can take place.

From here, once again individuals just live with the conditions set forth in their lives. That is until they reach the age of 43, or near that age, then the part of life known as 'Mid-life-crises,' comes into play. Again they live with things the way they are but it is now understood that they can make a change if they want to, and if a change is coming it will take place between the ages of 56 and 59.

After this age there is another low point about the age of 74, and most often people just understand it is too late to make another major change in life so they learn to live with their current lifestyle. A contributing factor at this age is the fact that the sexual drive is also beginning to wane so any drive to change mates is soon forgotten.

LIFE CHANGING MOON'S NODAL RETURNS

You will find the moon, or its nodal positions, have a great deal of influence in the lives of all things. However, the cycles of the Moon's nodes are the ones of greater importance to the human being.

These are the nodal return locations that take place in life. Individually it will be best if a person has a natal birth chart so that they can observe it as the moon's orbit around the earth takes place.

The more prominent years in most peoples lives, that are affected by the moon's nodes, or nodal returns, are ages 19, 38, 57 and 76. You will notice that the age 57 nodal influence is also involved with the Uranus cycle that brings new beginnings at age 56, 57. When a person passes through the first house again for the second time in life, and on the Uranus cycle during their life time.

LIFE INSURANCE SALES

Records for this 9.03 year cycle have been kept since 1858 and are continuing still. This is a cycle that the insurance companies pay close attention to. It seems as though the higher sales happen when the Moon's transiting node is trine to the US charts North node at 7° Leo. The lower sales take place more often when the transiting Node is semi-sextile to the North nodal location. You must remember that insurance is often a guilt product. You will see advertisements saying something like the following. "Don't you want to protect your family in case of your death?" In a sense this is emotional blackmail.

LUNAR PHASES

PHASES	Northern Hemisphere	Southern Hemisphere
Darkened Moon	Not Visible	Not visible
New Moon	No visibility, or traditionally the first visible moon's crescent	
Waxing Crescent Moon	Right 1-49% visibility	Left 1-49% visibility
First Quarter	Right 50% visibility	Left 50% visibility
Waxing Gibbous	Right 51-99% visibility	Left 51-99% visibility
Full Moon	Fully visibility	Fully visibility
Waning Gibbous	Left 51-99% visibility	Right 51-99% visibility
Last Quarter	Left 50% visibility	Right 50% visibility
Waning Crescent Moon	Left 1-49% visibility	Right 1-49% visibility

MASS EXCITEMENT CYCLE
So named by a Soviet professor A.C. Tchyivsky.
Shortly after world war one he found that
throughout history events such as migrations,
crusades or uprisings and revolutions, even war,
seems to occur more often when the sun is near
its peak sunspot cycle.

This cycle runs a gamut of four parts. The first
three-year period starts out slowly and
characterized by peaceful tolerances of those we
do not agree with. Because if our passive nature
we lack unity, and are largely led by the seemingly
needs of minorities.

Then there is a two-year period in which the
masses begin to feel more needs and with this the
excitabilities begin to grow. New leaders with a
mind bordering on revolution start to emerge, they
in turn challenge the concepts and reasoning of
those who hold positions of power at the time.
Often these same new leaders have no real
alliance or direction, and they may be fueled by
the media and what is found in print, or on the
news.

The third period is three years and is the one
where the greatest danger to mankind is
encountered. This is the time for wars, riots, and
conflicts that involve bloody deaths are a common
occurrence.

This does result in better social reforms being put into place as this time passes. The fourth period is also one of three years and brings gradual decreases in human excitability. To the point that the masses become almost lethargic and they cry out for peace in the lands. Now they lie like sleeping bears in hibernation, awaiting the next cycle to begin yet again.

MARRIAGE CYCLES

These 18.2 year cycles are very interesting from two different points of view. First the amount of marriages taking place go up and down with the Moon's nodes. Prior to my research, what I found in the USA, were marital highs in 1869, 1881, 1891, 1896, 1923, 1945. And that fewer marriages took place in 1876, 1897, 1915, 1932, 1951. Marriage cycles have been studied since 1867, but mostly in the USA. However, the cycle presented here should have the same results internationally as well.

Then there are our own personal marriage cycles. These too have an 18.2 year cycle. The Moon's nodal returns can be used to track this cycle in the individuals natal chart. As it happens many marriages fall apart after 18.2 years even when they seem to be on solid foundations. Marriage involves the seventh house of partners, and look to Venus for the involvement of love affairs outside the marriage.

MENSTRUAL CYCLES

Traditional sources agree that the menstrual cycle is linked to the cycle of the moon. It is not the light of the moon that has the effect, but the moon's influence as a celestial body.

In Astrology it is simple to find the moon's position and constellation it inhabits at the time of a woman's birth, this knowledge will tell you when her natural cycle will take affect.

I've found that when the transiting moon each month enters the sign that has the most prominent influence in a woman's first house, it may trigger her menstrual cycle. The two Lunar cycles that have an effect on us as humans, are 27 ½ days by constellation, and 29 ½ days by phase. You may want to consider the moon's nodes in her chart as well. The moon also takes close to 28 days to revolve around the Earth (Actually 27.32 days). The synodical lunar month, the period between two new moons (or full moons), is 29.53 days long. Apparently it has been suggested that artificial lighting may have some influence in disturbing the normal lunar cycle. These cycles are considered normal when they start at age12 and normally continue until age 45 to 55. By the age of 43 it is believed that most women can no longer have children, at least without help from a fertility clinic. The decline in fertility rates is attributed to sun spot cycles.

MENTALITY

These are cycles that are rarely considered, but it can be useful information to be aware of. The highs and lows average 6.8 to 7.0 years apart and start at birth. The first low is at birth and the first high is at age seven. The basic table is as follows.

Lows	Highs
Birth	7
14	21
28	35
42	49
56	63
70	77

Once the age of seventy-seven is reached, you must also remember that old age is becoming a factor that affects a person's memory. This normal mental condition may now change as to what was the high and low points. In this part of the cycle the mentality of an individual can change where there are periods of time where lucidity is questionable.

There is a form that doctors use to help determine the memory status in their patients and is known as the MMSE form.

MERCURY

The planet Mercury produces some interesting cycles in the lives of human beings, though they may possibly go un-noticed by most people. It is the retrograde condition that is the more interesting. The retrograde condition of Mercury takes place three or four times a year. Those of us with the ability to create things, whether mental, or visual, are able to see Mercury's affect more often than most others. As this is a condition that seems to shut down the creative way of thinking. See the section on 'Writer's Block.'

METAL PRODUCTION

The production of metal has been a long term study, such as Aluminum production has records going back to 1885, and has a cycle of 6.0 to 6.4 years. Metal is associated with the planet Mars, but the cycle seems to be connected to the Moon's nodal transit. In comparing the highs and lows of production.

According to the natal chart on the United States of America, the high production rates take place when the transiting moon's node is trine to the north node in the US chart. The low production rates are when the transiting moon's node is trine, or semi-sextile to the US charts south node.

METONIC CYCLE

This is a 19.0 year cycle which measures the recurrence of New Moons at nearly the same degree of the constellation it is in at the time. Though it is close to the nodal cycle of 18.6 years, it is different. It is also an eclipse cycle which only lasts for about 4 or 5 eclipses. These are recorded on a regular basis by such organizations as the American Federation of Astrologers.

MICE

The high and low points, on mouse population, are four years apart, and this is equal to a nodal Square. When you determine the highest mouse, or mice, population, the next low point predicted will be about four years later. It can actually run closer to four and a half years.

MID-LIFE CRISIS
For years personal life counselors, Phychiratists and Psychoanalysts of every sort have tried to figure out why people have a mid-fife crisis at 42, 43 years of age. I will explain here, but briefly, for a more detailed explanation you can read the section on Uranus Cycles.'

The mid-life crisis comes when the planet Uranus has reached a point in its orbit which is opposite to the natal location it was in at the time of a persons birth. Here it reacts in opposition to what is good for the individual. It is rebellion, simple as that.

MOON
Most people never give the influence the moon has in their lives a second thought.
They know that there is going to be a high and low tide twice a day and they just accept these kind of things that take place because they have always been that way. However, the moon has a tremendous affect on their lives, an affect that would astound them were they aware of its real power. The placement of the moon above, or below the elliptical plane at the time of their birth, is its nodal position, and it is a very important factor to understand.

MOON'S NODES BY AGE

All things have a beginning such as your birth, and that is where you begin your cycle count. Use that as a starting point as a time of birth, which includes the beginning of any life, even seasons, or crops being planted.

The Moon has what is known as Nodal ages. They start at the beginning, or birth of any event, and take place as marked points in the cycles, or the ages of the cycle. Those ages as points in time are as follows. 3, 6, 9, 12, 15, 19, 22, 25, 28, 31, 34, 38, 41, 44, 47, 50, 53, 57, 60, 63, 66, 69, 72, 76, 79, 82, 85, 88, 91, and 95.

If you create, or draw, a circle of 360 degrees, and representing the Moon's orbit around the earth, put a dot somewhere on that line to represent the moon, you can use it to map the nodal ages through its progression by age. You will see that every time it moves to a point 60 degrees from the last age point, it is of a new age.

Considering its point of beginning you look for the first age to happen at a sextile aspect of 30 degrees. The next one is at a trine, 120 degrees, then the opposition of 180 degrees. On the return you pass through another trine, then a sextile, finally back to the beginning, or a conjunction.

NEW BEGINNINGS

Every 29.2 years we, as human beings go in new, and often entirely different directions in our lives. This can be a decision that is often hard to make at the time, but we do it, and more often than not, are better off for having done so. This is a cycle that repeats every 29.2 years. The second time is at the age of 56. The first time this change is made often brings a struggle period for the following seven years. If corrections to the lifestyle are made the first time, the second change at age 56 will be much easier and the following seven years will not be as hard a struggle. The New Beginning cycle is triggered as a part of the Uranus cycle.

NODAL RETURNS

The returning of the Moon to its nodal position at the time of birth, or beginning of an event, is a cycle that is found in almost all things in life and is perhaps one of the most important cycles to study.

As an example when you find the Moon's nodal position in any constellation, you will find it has returned to that position nine years and three or four months later. Without question the pull of the moon in our lives is of paramount importance and anyone who discounts this is simply ignorant of the facts.

They are called the north, or south, nodes depending upon the moons' relationship to its elliptical plane. The elliptical plane is an imaginary horizontal line drawn between the Sun and the Earth.

When the moon, in its orbit around the earth, crosses over this line it changes from one node to the other. When it is above this line, it is listed as a northern nodal position and as it crosses below the line it is listed as being in a southern nodal position.

Astrological history tells us that the Moon's north node in a natal chart marks the beginning of things, and the south node is the end result.

PLANETARY ORBITS

To some this section may not hold anything of
interest, but those who wish to research avenues
of interest to them, may find the following
planetary information of use. Normally we do not
think of the planets in orbit around our sun, and
having cycles. But, in reality, that is exactly what
they are, cycles.

There are many who do not, or cannot admit to
the fact that the planets have an influence on
mankind. When you consider that at the center of
our galaxy there is a black hole that is so powerful
that even light cannot escape its influence. This
same black hole exerts enough magnetic pull so
as to keep the rest of our galaxy in its place. This
of course includes our Sun and our own solar
system.

Planet	Rotation Periods	Planetary Orbital period
Sun	25 D, 9H, 7M, 11.6 S 25.05 D at Equator 34.3 D at poles	225-250 Mi8llion Yrs
Moon	27D, 7H, 43M, 11.5S	24 Hrs
Mercury	58D, 15H, 30M, 30S	0.24 Yr - 87.969D
Venus	243D, 0H, 26M	0.62 Yr - 224.7D

Mars   1 D, 0H, 37M, 22.663 M   1.88 Yr - 1Y, 322D
                                  It rotates 3.2 times
                                  Each time it orbits
                                  the sun

Ceres   0H, 9H, 4M, 27.0 M   0.38D - 4.60Y

Jupiter 9H, 55M, 29.37S interior 11.86 Yr - 11Y, 314D
        9H, 50M, 30S Equator
        9H, 55M, 43.63S High Latitude

Saturn 10H, 39M, 24S Interior   29.46 Yr - 29Y, 167D
        10H, 14M Equator
        10H, 38M High Latitude

Uranus 17H, 14M, 24S   84.01Yr - 84Y

Neptune 16H, 6M, 36S   164.8 Yr - 164Y, 167D

Pluto   6D, 9H, 17M, 32S   248.09Y

PLANKTON
The rise and fall of Plankton seems to change on the nodal square. However, it is also dependent upon other factors as well, such as the La Nina or El Ninio warming of the oceans.

RAILROADS
In the past most railroad companies were somewhat seasonal as to the tonnage they moved across the country. To some degree they still are, but the onset of the oil crisis caused more merchandise to be shipped by rail instead of by trucks for the long haul. In 1942 the Canadian Pacific Railway had their chief Statistician, G. Meridith Roundtree start a study for their business fluctuations. He began with records dating back to 1903, he found a 9.18 month cycle with forty-nine repetitions. My research shows the Moon's nodes were to be found more in the water signs on the higher trends, which is trine to the US natal charts Cancer planets in the eighth house. Also, some were found to be in the fire signs which is conjunct, or trine, to the US natal charts fourth house of home, and trine or conjunct to the US natal charts North node.

REAL ESTATE SALES CYCLES

It's hard to believe that records for the sale of real-estate were started so long ago, but they were being recorded as early as 1795. You can use the US Chart to measure the highs and lows of the land market fluctuations starting with the known date of Feb 1795. The cycle I found that fits the dates of each high and low real-estate market from that time, are the Moon's Nodal returns. Those dates are as follows, and I've extended the future of the cycle out to the year 2037.

The Transiting
Moon's Node   Conjunction / Opposition The USA chart's

Moons Nodes   Market Condition & Date

Moons Nodes			Date	Market
North - Conjunction to North Leo		2 / 14 / 1795	High
Opposition to	South	Aquarius	6 / 6 / 1804	Low
Conjunction to	North		9 / 26 / 1813	High
Opposition to	South		1 / 17 / 1823	Low
Conjunction to	North		5 / 8 / 1832	High
Opposition to	South		8 / 28 / 1841	Low
Conjunction to	North		12 /18 / 1850	High
Opposition to	South		4 / 8 / 1860	Low
Conjunction to	North		7 / 29 / 1869	High
Opposition to	South		11 / 19 / 1878	Low
Conjunction to	North		3 / 10 / 1888	High
Opposition to	South		6 / 30 / 1897	Low
Conjunction to	North		10 / 21 / 1906	High
Opposition to	South		2 / 10 / 1916	Low
Conjunction to	North		6 / 1 / 1925	High
Opposition to	South		9 / 22 / 1934	Low
Conjunction to	North		1 / 15 / 1944	High
Opposition to	South		5 / 3 / 1953	Low

Conjunction	to	North	8 / 23 / 1962	High
Opposition	to	South	12 / 19 / 1971	Low
Conjunction	to	North	4 / 3 / 1981	High
Opposition	to	South	7 / 24 / 1990	Low
Conjunction	to	North	11 / 14 / 1999	High
Opposition	to	South	3 / 27 / 2009	Low
Conjunction	to	North	5 / 29 / 2018	High
Opposition	to	South	5 / 29 / 2018	Low
Conjunction	to	North	10 / 27 / 2027	High
Opposition	to	South	3 / 3 / 2037	Low

SALES CYCLES

The 6 year cycles for sales are found to be connected to the Sun spot cycles. The highest activity of sun spots takes place every eleven years, plus or minus. The sales cycles fluctuate when the sun spots reach a high point, and a low point. See the 'Sun spot cycles', for dates of the highest activity.

SALMON CYCLES

The Restigouche Salmon club in Canada has kept records of the abundance of Salmon since 1880. They established a continuous cycle of the highs and lows of Salmon runs on the Restigouche river that runs between the Gaspe Peninsula and New Brunswick. They found the cycle is repetitive and averages 9.6 years between the high points. Some of those high years are, 1885, 1895, 1905, 1916, 1924, 1933, 1943, and 1951. Though my research, as yet, has not established the conditions in those years, it is no doubt lunar related.

SATURN CYCLES

The influence of this planet in the human lifestyle is probably one of the more important, and often overlooked. Though it does not have a good reputation, it is one of the more revealing planets in the field of Astrology. By age its cycles are as follows.

High	Low
Birth	14.71 years
29.42 years	44.13 years
58.84 years	73.55 years
88.26 years	102.97 years

Perhaps the most important of these cycles is when the Saturn influence comes into play as other planetary cycles are also active in a persons life at the same time. Two of the more influential time periods in the younger years are at the ages of 29.42 years, and 44.13 years. These years correspond to changes that take place with the presence of the Uranus cycle. The planet Uranus brings changes of any kind, but with Saturn involved the changes that take place is normally that of the subconscious mind cleaning up mental baggage.

SEXUAL CRAVINGS

The sex drive is normally more intensified each month when the transiting moon passes through the constellation that Venus was in at the time of a person's birth, and can be observed by consulting someone's natal horoscopic chart. The moon returns to this location on the average of every 28 days. The intensity will be transmitted through the sign / constellation, and house it appears in. In an individual's natal chart the strongest sexual need is when Venus is found in the first house, the house of physical being. When Venus is found in the first house is often where you find someone who suffers from sexual addiction. This will depend on the constellation Venus is in, and its relationship to the other planets.

SEXUAL ADVERTISING

The gap in life, formed by a lack of complete sexual fulfilment, is one that finds its way onto the internet, and in a big way. People looking for other people are commonly found in several locations in the internet realm. I was surprised when I first began to look into these sites, as I found the more common age, though not the only one for those responding, and looking for someone, falls between the ages of 28 to 33.

This does not include the predatory types, only those who have an immediate need for their age group, and this is the more prevalent age group although there others. The first age group comes into play because of the combination of the Uranus cycle at the age of 28 and the first return of Saturn in the person's life. This planetary combination brings about the search for a new direction in life. The second age group, 42, 43, takes place when the mid-life crisis comes into play. There is a lunar connection as well. Also, a Uranus influence can often found. The person who advertises usually does so when the moon transits over their natal Venus.

SEXUAL PREDATORS

The cyclic behavior of these individuals is affected by the moon's transit through the sign that the planet Venus is in at the time of their birth. There are indications that this kind of addiction comes with those born between Late September, and mid April. The more common signs for the planet Venus to inhabit one of the signs of Scorpio, Capricorn, Aquarius, or Aries. It is the placement in a person's birth chart for this planet, and its relationship to the other planets and their houses at the time of birth, that bring out this predatory kind of individual. The planet Mars, or planets in the constellation of Aries, will most often be influential in this persons' sexual drive. As to how it plays out can be indicated by the other planets in aspect to these locations.

SOLAR RADIATION

There is a solar radiation cycle that affects earth and appears to take place every 7.58 years. Solar radiation is also tied to sun spot activity.

STOCK PRICES

First of all you must understand that the stock market is in reality a group of people who are, in essence, gamblers. They are betting that this stock, or that one, is going to go up or down in sales. With this in mind, I could not find a correlation to the US chart other than there seems to be some various differences in potential when the Moon's North Node is in the fire signs, Aries, Leo or Sagittarius, also the earth signs, Taurus, Virgo, or Capricorn.

However, a 9.2 year cycle is without question a Lunar cycle. There is also a 4.5 year cycle, and one of 41 months. The heaviest events, up or down, occurred in the following years. Oct 6. 1819, May 10 -1837, Sept 24, 1869, Jan 19 1882, Panic 1884, Panic 1886, Panic 1901, Panic 1907, Oct 1929, US 1937, 1963, UK 1973, Oct 1987, Oct 1989, UK 1992, Asia 1997, and Oct, Nov. of 2008. In the long run it has been found that there are thirty-seven potential cycles, or trends, in the stock market.

SUICIDE

A contributing factor that may be found involved is that when the ending of one's life by self murder, is often found to be Mars, as the aggressive planet. The Moon as the emotional catalyst, and perhaps any one of these transiting the first or twelfth house of the natal chart. The self caused death happens more in the month of June than any other time. Of course this is the month of the Moon, and emotions may run more rampant at this time of year than any other.

SUN

The Sun's orbit through the 'Milky Way' galaxy takes about 225 to 250 million years. It orbits the center at a distance of 26,000, or 27,000 light years from the galactic center. This comes out to a passage equal to one light year every 1,190 years. It takes nearly 2160 years for the sun to complete a retrograde through each of the twelve zodiacal constellations and is known as a solar age. It takes 25, 920 years for the precession of the equinoxes through the twelve constellations.

An oddity about the sun that stymies scientists is that the sun rotates faster at the equator than it does at the higher latitudes of its solar body. At the equator it makes one rotation in 25 days, while at latitude 75 degrees it takes thirty one days to complete a rotation. There is some who think the magnetic fields between our sun and the planets in our solar system effect the sun's equator speed. Like our moon that causes the tides to rise as our planet turns with the moon in orbit around us. However, the drag of the water moving in a tidal form on earth causes some friction and this in turn is slowing the rotation of our earth on its axis.

SUN'S POLARITY

It is a known fact that the sun has some instability in its core. With fluctuations taking place between 41,000 to 100,000 years.

Of interest is the Mayan calender that ends on September 22, of 2012. It is thought that this is the date that the Sun is to change its magnetic poles. The sun's polar reversal is a known and recorded history and has not affected earth according to available written history. In the year of 2009, there was some question as to the Suns' normal behavior. It should have started a new cycle which would have included a new series of sunspots, but it seems as if it did not do this as was expected. The question arose as, "Is it getting ready to change polarity earlier than expected? Read the section on Sunspot cycles. The sun"s last magnetic pole change happened last in 627 AD.

SUNSPOTS

Interestingly, though the cycles average eleven years in length, in the seventeenth century there was very little activity in sunspots. This coincides with the Little Ice Age. This period is known as the Maunder Minimum. Sun spots have been reported as far back as 28BC, but were first observed with a telescope in 1610 by Thomas Harriot, an English Astronomer.

If you think our sun is unusual, you would be mistaken. In 1947, GE Kron observed sun spots from Red Dwarf stars in other galaxies, only then they were called 'star spots. In Mid 2009 a television show done on our Sun, indicated that there was some interest in the fact that the sunspots were not taking place as expected, that the sun seemed to be quieter than normal as if something else were going on.

Read the section on the 'Sun's Polarity.' The sun spot cycle runs 11.1 years, but it also has a cycle that brings its magnetic fields back to the beginning placement every 87.45 days, and it does the same thing every 187 years. The Mayan calendar was founded on sunspot cycles.

Listed Sun Spot cycles:
March 1755 - June 1766
June 1766 - September 1784
September 1784 - May 1798
May 1798 - December 1810
December 1810 - May 1823
May 1823 - November 1833
November 1833 - July 1843
July 1843 - December 1855
December 1855 - March 1867
March 1867 - December 1878
December 1878 - March 1890
March 1890 - February 1902
February 1902 - August 1913
August 1913 - August 1923
August 1923 - September 1933
September 1933 - February 1944
February 1944 - April 1954
April 1954 - October 1964
October 1964 - June 1976
June 1976 - September 1986
September 1986 - May 1996
May 1996 - Perhaps this one won't finish
until 2008, or 200

TIRE SHREDDING

This is one of those things that normally go unnoticed. People see pieces of retread tires littering our highways, but think little of it. Still, over time I began to wonder why those pieces of rubber were not showing up on a continual basis. I looked first at Neptune because it is associated with rubber, but it is too slow in its orbit to be involved with the faster cycle of tires being shredded along the highways of the world. The research on this cycle is still young, but I have found it often takes place when the moon's north node is going into a retrograde condition.

TRAVELING

The moon's nodal location is almost always a contributing factor in things that happen in our lives. Traveling is no exception. If you travel when the Moon's Nodes are in a conjunction, a square, or an opposition to the Sun during your travels, you will often become aware of more accidents, perhaps more violence, or natural disasters taking place. If the Moon's nodes are in Taurus, Virgo, or Capricorn, and in a critical part of your chart, it may not be a good time for you to travel. These events take place three or four times a year.

Retrograde Mercury also plays a part in traveling. When it is at its Apogee, the furthest point away from the sun and in its orbit around the Sun, it has the largest effect on mankind. It will affect each person differently, but in general it causes problems with your hotel or motel room booking, paperwork mistakes and unusual tie ups in traffic, or delays of any kind. Though they won't necessarily know why, but hospitals will tell you they seem to have cycles of people coming in for injured toes, fingers about three of four times a year. It is during retrograde Mercury that this happens.

TREES

Can you use a tree to power your house, not likely? However, strange as it may seem, trees have an ongoing electrical current passing through them. If you had a meter that was sensitive enough, you might be able to read how much. To do this you would have to drill two very small holes about three or so feet apart in the tree's trunk. Push one end of a wire into each hole and an electric current will flow along the wire. The voltage of the current will change from time to time and it will also change direction. The change in direction will happen about every six months. It will be the same condition in other trees of the same kind, yet miles apart from one another. Tree rings have been found to change in a cycle similar to that of the sun spot cycles.

URANUS CYCLES

The Uranus cycle is one of the more interesting cycles, mostly because of its long term effect in the lives of humans. Some segments of the entire 84 year cycle, are as short as 2.3 years. The next segment is 7.0 years in length and each of those seven year segments will have a different effect in the lives of humanity. There are also three 28.0 year segments. When a person reaches the end of first 28.0 year cycle, they will find a dramatic change in their attitude and outlook on life as they make a major adjustment in their lives. The second 28.0 year cycle, which ends at age 56, will also bring a change, but not as dramatically as the first one. To trace this cycle in life, you need to understand some basics about a person's natal birth chart. It consists of twelve houses representing the twelve constellations of the Zodiac. You begin with the cusp of the first house, and allot two years four months of time to each house. Continuing around the houses in numerical order until the age of 84 has been completed. This will represent one orbit of the planet Uranus in our solar system.

WAR CYCLES
The lengths of which range from 142 years, 57 year, 22.3 year, 17.71 years, 17.31 years, 11.28 years, 9.6 years, and 5.98 years, and those are the more average cycles.

It seems the chance of getting through a year with absolute peaceful conditions, and without a warlike condition, are one in seventeen. Also, it seems, that there is a correlation to droughts and civil wars that evolve on a 170 year cycle as well as a 510 year cycle.

There have been studies of these cycles that begin with the year AD 1100. Prior to that between the years of 600 BC to AD 900, the cycle averaged 163.5 years. The 17.71 year cycle seems to be determined on an economic need of those involved. There are many who wonder if mankind ever learn that war is a complete waste of human life and that in the long run it serves no positive attribute. Or, that will we simply annihilate ourselves before it becomes a lesson learned where only those few survivors understand the error of our ways.

Highest war years.
The following years include the 142, 57, 22.5, and 11.5 years war cycles.
1100, 1250, 1360, 1420, 1454, 1470, 1498, 1520, 1527, 1538, 1560, 1582, 1610, 1625, 1656, 1678, 1708, 1718, 1740, 1755, 1761, 1776, 1782, 1790, 1793, 1798, 1801, 1808, 1813, 1824, 1830, 1839, 1840, 1849, 1854, 1862,3, 1878, 1892, 1804, 1817, 1898, 1902, 1914, 1932, 1910, 1918, 1939, 1944, 1950.

The United States through history has found itself becoming involved in war conditions, or ending one, when the planet Mars and Uranus come into a conjunction.

WEATHER CYCLES

These cycles vary. Here are but a few of the basic weather cycles, 4.3 years, 7.6 years, 100 years. Apparently the 100 year cycle is the one of the most important. It should not be of a surprise to people in the United States to find a weather calendar issued yearly, it has been known since its beginning as 'The Farmer's Almanac.' You too can produce nearly the same thing for your own area of any part of the world if you do a little research. Keep notes on the weather on a daily basis for a good length of time for your area, and on each change of the weather look to see what constellation the moon is transiting. To have this data at your disposal will indicate what you can expect in the future. Basically, if the Moon is passing through the fire signs, Aries, Leo and Sagittarius you can expect good weather for those days. If the Moon is passing through the water signs, Cancer, Scorpio, or Pisces, you can expect damp weather, such as rain or fog, snow, etc. When it is passing through the Earth signs, Taurus, Virgo, or Capricorn, it may be Muggy, oppressive, cloudy, suffocating heat where you seek the shade. These conditions will have to be altered according to the time of year, but will still reflect the basic weather effects. Still, why does it rain on January 23 in Brisbane, Australia?

WHEAT PRICES

Lord Beveridge began tracking the prices of wheat in 1500, and published his results in his 'Periodogram.' The perfect cycle is 54 years, but that is often modified by other factors. You can find records on this subject in English history dating from 1259. In my research I found that the two planets' Uranus and Saturn seemed to be found in the air or water signs during the market highs, the air signs being the more prominent for the more prominent high points. The low periods find the same two planets in the fire and earth signs, the fire signs being the more prominent.

WRITER'S BLOCK
These conditions happen three or four times yearly. The cycle for these periods of time in a creative person's life is a common cycle, but largely misunderstood. The mental block that takes place in these cycles' effect each person differently, so it is best for those who are aware of these cycles to make notes about how things take place for them during these time periods.

Writers' block can be tracked by observing the planet Mercury and its retrograde condition. Generally the first week of the retrograde condition, brings an absence of mental creativity, it's as if the mind has shut down. This is a time when most writers do their rewriting of previously written material, work than only takes some mental sorting through.

The second week some mental stimulus begins to take place and the mental creativity may begin to give a few new ideas.

The third week the mind may seem overwhelmed with new thoughts on how to bring the creative fruition to some kind of completeness.

Writers often make notes about the many thoughts that come to mind during this third week. Then, when they need some new project they go to this list to view their notes on newer thoughts for a writing project. Those who find Mercury going retrograde in their Sun sign, or the constellation from which their artistic abilities emanate, will be the most affected by this event.

PLANETARY RESEARCH INFORMATION

For those who wish to continue researching cycles that may be affected by a particular planet, I will include this additional orbital data.

SUN

The sun returns to the same location every 19.0 years

Sun's duration = .083 hours per house and the orbit is 365 Days 7 Hrs. Mean average, but does not consider retrograde conditions

0° Aries to 0° Taurus - 30 days = 4 wks 2 days = 30° Semi-sextile

0° Aries to 0° Gemini - 60 days = 8 wks 4 days = 60° Sextile

0° Aries to 0° Cancer - 90 days = 12 wks 6 days = 90° Square

0° Aries to 0° Leo - 120 days = 16 wks 8 days = 120° Trine

0° Aries to 0° Virgo - 150 days = 20 wks 10 days = 150° Quincunx

0° Aries to 0° Libra - 180 days = 24 wks 12 days = 180° Opposition

0° Aries to 0° Scorpio - 210 days = 28 wks 14 days = 150° Quincunx

0° Aries to 0° Sagittarius - 240 days = 32 wks 16 days = 120° Trine

0° Aries to 0° Capricorn -270 days = 36 wks 18 days = 90° Square

0° Aries to 0° Aquarius - 300 days = 40 wks 20 days = 60° Sextile

0° Aries to 0° Pisces -328 days = 44 wks 20 days = 30° Semi-sextile

0° Aries to 0° Aries -358 days = 48 wks 22 days = Conjunction

MOON
The Moon returns to the same location every 4.0 years, however the moon is retrograde for 3.0 minutes a day. If a nodal return is within 3.0° of a planets position, it will have an effect on the moon's influence.

Moons nodal returns are 18.2 years, or 9.1 years to an opposition. Many cycles are in conjunction with these two positions of the moon at the time of any birth. However, this basic cycle is known to have an effect on other things when it reaches a square aspect to that of birth as well. This would be a 4.5 +\- year cycle.

Moon = 2.3 days per house, or sign - Orbit is 28 Days. A mean average, but does not consider retrograde conditions

0° Aries to 0° Taurus - 2.3 days - 30° Semi-sextile

0° Aries to 0° Gemini - 4.6 days - 60° Sextile

0° Aries to 0° Cancer - 6.9 days - 90° Square

0° Aries to 0° Leo - 8.2 days - 120° Trine

0° Aries to 0° Virgo - 10.5 days - 150° Quincunx

0° Aries to 0° Libra - 12.8 days - 180° Opposition

0° Aries to 0° Scorpio - 15.1 days - 150° Quincunx

0° Aries to 0° Sagittarius - 17.4 days - 120° Trine

0° Aries to 0° Capricorn - 19.7 days - 90° Square

0° Aries to 0° Aquarius - 22 days - 60° Sextile

0° Aries to 0° Pisces - 24.3 days - 30° Semi-sextile

0° Aries to 0° Aries - 26.6 days - Conjunction

MERCURY

Mercury crosses the elliptical plane on average every seven years. Its retrograde condition takes place three of four times a year. Mercury returns to the same location every 10.0 years

Mercury = 7.3 days per house - Orbit is 88 Days

Mercury = 7.6 Months to a retrograde position
A mean average, but does not consider retrograde conditions

0° Aries to 0° Taurus - 15 days - 30° Semi-sextile

0° Aries to 0° Gemini - 29 day - 60° Sextile
Average length of Retrograde

0° Aries to 0° Cancer - 45 days - 90° Square
is 22 days

0° Aries to 0° Leo - 59 days - 120° Trine

0° Aries to 0° Virgo - 76 days - 150° Quincunx

0° Aries to 0° Libra - 92 days - 180° Opposition

0° Aries to 0° Scorpio - 110 days - 150° Quincunx

0° Aries to 0° Sagittarius - 129 days - 120° Trine

0° Aries to 0° Capricorn - 148 days - 90° Square

0° Aries to 0° Aquarius -168 days - 60° Sextile

0° Aries to 0° Pisces - 186 days - 30° Semi-sextile

VENUS
Venus returns to the same location every 8.0 years
Venus goes retrograde on average of six times every ten years.
Venus = 18.6 days per house - Orbit is 224 Days. A mean average, but does not consider retrograde conditions.

0° Aries to 0° Taurus - 25 days - 30° Semi-sextile

0° Aries to 0° Gemini - 49 days - 60° Sextile
Average length of Retrograde

0° Aries to 0° Cancer - 73 days - 90° Square
is 42 says

0° Aries to 0° Leo - 99 days - 120° Trine

0° Aries to 0° Virgo - 124 days - 150° Quincunx

0° Aries to 0° Libra - 148 days - 180° Opposition

0° Aries to 0° Scorpio - 172 days - 150° Quincunx

0° Aries to 0° Sagittarius - 196 days - 120° Trine

0° Aries to 0° Capricorn - 220 days - 90° Square

0° Aries to 0° Aquarius -244 days - 60° Sextile
0° Aries to 0° Pisces - 264 days - 30° Semi-sextile

JUPITER
Jupiter returns to the same location every 12.0 years.
Jupiter = 360.75 days per house -12 Months - Orbit is 11 Years 314 Days
Jupiter = 7.6 months to a squared position
A mean average, but does not consider retrograde conditions.

0° Aries to 0° Taurus - 360.75 days - 30° Semi-sextile

0° Aries to 0° Gemini - 721.5 days - 60° Sextile

0° Aries to 0° Cancer - 1082.25 days - 90° Square

0° Aries to 0° Leo - 1443 days - 120° Trine

0° Aries to 0° Virgo - 1803 days - 150° Quincunx

0° Aries to 0° Libra - 2164.5 - 180° Opposition

0° Aries to 0° Scorpio - 2886 days - 150° Quincunx

0° Aries to 0° Sagittarius - 3607.5 - 120° Trine

0° Aries to 0° Capricorn -3968.25 - 90° Square

0° Aries to 0° Aquarius - 4329 days - 60° Sextile

0° Aries to 0° Pisces - 4689.75 days - 30° Semi-sextile

SATURN

Saturn returns to the same location every 30.0 years.

Saturn = 1075.2 days per house- 25 +/- mths

Orbit is 29 Years 167 Days

A mean average, but does not consider retrograde conditions.

0° Aries to 0° Taurus - 153.6 wks - ° Semi-sextile

0° Aries to 0° Gemini - 60° Sextile 4/21/01 @ 0° Gemini = 2Y, 1M, 1 W

0° Aries to 0° Cancer - 90° Square 6/06/03 @ 0° Cancer = 2 Y, 1M, 1W 4D

0° Aries to 0° Leo -120° Trine 7/17/05 @ 0° Leo = 2Y, 1M, 2W, 2D

0° Aries to 0° Virgo -150° Quincunx 9/03/07 @ 0° Virgo = 2Y, 10M, 2W, 5D

0° Aries to 0° Libra -180° Opposition 7/22/10 @ 0° Libra

0° Aries to 0° Scorpio -150° Quincunx 10/06/12 @ 0° Scorpio

0° Aries to 0° Sagittarius -120° Trine 12/24/14 @ 0° Sagittarius

0° Aries to 0° Capricorn - 90° Square 12/21/17 @ 0° Capricorn

0° Aries to 0° Aquarius - 60° Sextile 12/17/20 @ 0° Aquarius

0° Aries to 0° Pisces - 30° Semi-sextile 3/08/23 @ 0° Pisces 5/26/25 @ 0° Aries

URANUS

Uranus returns to the same location every 90.0 years

Uranus = Averages 2 Years 4 Months per house - 196 wks, = 49 M, 4.08 Y

 Orbit is 84 Years and averages - 7 years per house. A mean average, but does not consider retrograde conditions

0° Aries to 0° Taurus - 7 Yrs - 30° Semi-sextile

0° Aries to 0° Gemini - 14 Yrs- 60° Sextile

0° Aries to 0° Cancer - 21 Yrs - 90° Square

0° Aries to 0° Leo - 28 Yrs - 120° Trine

0° Aries to 0° Virgo - 35 Yrs - 150° Quincunx

0° Aries to 0° Libra - 42 Yrs - 180° Opposition

0° Aries to 0° Scorpio - 49 Yrs - 150° Quincunx

0° Aries to 0° Sagittarius - 56 Yrs - 120° Trine

0° Aries to 0° Capricorn - 63 Yrs - 90° Square

0° Aries to 0° Aquarius - 70 Yrs - 60° Sextile

0° Aries to 0° Pisces - 77 Yrs - 30° Semi-sextile

0° Aries to 0° Aries - 84 Yrs - Conjunction to point of return

NEPTUNE
Neptune returns to the same location every 180.0 years. Neptune = 6,0027.0 days per house - Orbit is 164 Years 167 Days
A mean average, but does not consider retrograde conditions

0° Aries to 0* Taurus - 30° Semi-sextile

0° Aries to 0* Gemini - 60° Sextile

0° Aries to 0* Cancer - 90° Square

0° Aries to 0* Leo -120° Trine

0° Aries to 0* Virgo - 150° Quincunx

0° Aries to 0* Libra -180° Opposition

0° Aries to 0* Scorpio -150° Quincunx

0° Aries to 0* Sagittarius -120° Trine

0° Aries to 0* Capricorn - 90° Square

0° Aries to 0* Aquarius - 60° Sextile

0° Aries to 0* Pisces - 30° Semi-sextile

PLUTO
Pluto = 9,0885.0 days per house - Orbit is 249
Years. A mean average, but does not consider
retrograde conditions

0° Aries to 0° Taurus - 30° Semi-sextile

0° Aries to 0° Gemini - 60° Sextile

0° Aries to 0° Cancer - 90° Square

0° Aries to 0° Leo - 120° Trine

0° Aries to 0° Virgo -150° Quincunx

0° Aries to 0° Libra -180° Opposition

0° Aries to 0° Scorpio -150° Quincunx

0° Aries to 0° Sagittarius -120° Trine

0° Aries to 0° Capricorn - 90° Square

0° Aries to 0° Aquarius - 60° Sextile

0° Aries to 0° Pisces - 30° Semi-sextile

ISIS

Isis = 14,0160.0 days per house - Orbit is 384 Years. A mean average, but does not consider retrograde conditions

0° Aries to 0° Taurus - 30° Semi-sextile

0° Aries to 0° Gemini - 60° Sextile

0° Aries to 0° Cancer - 90° Square

0° Aries to 0° Leo - 120° Trine

0° Aries to 0° Virgo - 150° Quincunx

0° Aries to 0° Libra - 180° Opposition

0° Aries to 0° Scorpio - 150° Quincunx

0° Aries to 0° Sagittarius - 120° Trine

0° Aries to 0° Capricorn - 90° Square

0° Aries to 0° Aquarius - 60° Sextile

0° Aries to 0° Pisces - 30° Semi-sextile

GLOSSARY

Constellations
Though there are many, the ones used as reference in this book are the more commonly known ones of Aries, Taurus, Gemini, Cancer, Leo, Virgo, Libra, Scorpio, Sagittarius, Capricorn, Aquarius and Pisces.

cycles
A cycle is an event that goes full circle, something that returns to its point of origin.

Declination
A planets declination is determined by its placement above or below the elliptical line. That is the imaginary line from the Sun to the center of our galaxy. It is either north, or south of this line in its orbit around the sun.

Elliptical plane
This is an imaginary line drawn from the sun to the center of our galaxy.

Nodal returns
Where ever the moon is at in its orbit around the earth should be noted when a new event takes place. This may be north, or south, of the elliptical plane, but its exact location can be found by consulting an ephemeris. It is when the moon returns to this same location that is known as the 'Nodal Return.'

Retrograde

This is a planetary condition relative to its orbit around the sun, or in case of the Moon, its orbit around earth. If a planet is nearing the end of its orbital oval loop around the sun, it slows in its travel speed. As it reaches the point where it is farthest from the sun, its apogee, it appears to slow in its orbital speed. This is the period where it is called, 'Retrograde.' As it picks up speed on its return closest to the Sun, its perigee, it is known as being. 'Direct' in motion.

Rhythms

A Rhythm is something that continues the same way each time, but may not return to the exact point of origin.

ISBN 1-882896-07-6
EAN 978-1-882896-07-3